IN THE GARDEN
WITH JESUS AND FRIENDS

A Practical Guidebook
for Helping Your Church
Develop a Fruit-bearing Ministry
in a Local Nursing Home

Chaplain Bill Goodrich

God Cares Ministry
Avon Lake, Ohio

ISBN: 978-0-9745384-6-4

All Scripture is taken from the HOLY BIBLE, NEW
INTERNATIONAL VERSION. NIV Copyright © 1973,
1978, 1984 by the International Bible Society. Used by
permission of the International Bible Society.

Some quotes in this guidebook were taken from <u>Nursing
Home Ministry – Where Hidden Treasures are Found,</u>
© 2003, 2005, 2009 Used with permission.

Published by
God Cares Ministry

515 Moore Road, Suite 3
Avon Lake, Ohio 44012
(440) 930-2173
www.GodCaresMinistry.com
info@GodCaresMinistry.com

*Dedicated to one of my most significant mentors,
Herm Haakenson,
who is now part of the welcome committee in
Heaven. I trust that those who follow the principles
in this guidebook will help to keep him busy.*

**Therefore, my brothers, be all the more eager to
make your calling and election sure. For if you do
these things, you will never fall,**

**and you will receive a rich welcome into the eternal
kingdom of our Lord and Savior Jesus Christ.**

2Peter 1:10-11

This is the second edition of this guidebook.
There have been some changes which have come
because I am always learning and seeking to
improve when possible. I am grateful for the
gracious support of friends who have contributed
to this edition.

Carolyn E. Altman
Pam Eck
Brian Scott
Arlene Sikorski

Illustrations are by Mary Ann Goodrich,
except for the one on the cover which is
by Paul Passano

I thank God for surrounding me with friends who care about my
friends. May our Lord Jesus continue to richly bless us as we
abide in Him! (John 15:1-17)

TABLE OF CONTENTS

INTRODUCTION

Several years ago I was among many ministry leaders displaying resources, and hoping to recruit a few people at an annual conference. This year was special, because the organizers asked if we would provide a break-out session for people interested in nursing home ministry. One of the people who attended this session was Lucy. She had been praying for the Lord to use her, but she was not quite sure where or what kind of ministry He would have her do. At the end of the session, Lucy was visibly excited and the following week she called my office reaffirming her desire to start a nursing home ministry in her church. I soon met with her pastor, and went over the basic steps needed to develop an effective ministry. Several weeks later, Lucy's team began their visits, and soon after, they began a weekly Bible study. This team continues to find great fulfillment, as do the residents in the home they adopted. Lucy has often expressed her gratitude for what God has done.

~ ~ ~ * ~ ~ ~

I had tried visiting in nursing homes on my own a couple of times with limited success. While the needs for ministry seemed overwhelming, finding help or advice was limited.

I had an old newsletter from God Cares Ministry, so, out of frustration, I called Bill Goodrich and told him what I was attempting to do. He replied, "that doesn't work, does it?" I told him "no." Then he began to explain what has been outlined in this guidebook, <u>In the Garden with Jesus and Friends</u>. It works!

That was seven years ago and now our church has a presence in three nursing homes. As a result of this, many nursing home residents have a home in heaven. Also, friendships with team members, residents, and staff have been made that will last for eternity.

Doug Feller, Trinity Evangelical Church, Amherst, Ohio

Lucy and Doug are the kind of people this guidebook was written for. They long to serve our Lord Jesus in a manner that brings glory to our Father in Heaven. They are believers who care, but need a helping hand to specifically express their faith and love toward neighbors who have true needs.

There is another kind of person this guidebook was written for, though she may never read it. Generally speaking, this person has lived a long life and had many hopes and dreams for enjoying the "golden years". But things did not go as planned. You see, something physically went wrong and now there is a need for 24 hour care in a long term nursing facility. She is hoping to get well and restart her life, but reality keeps knocking on her door to convince her that this is her life's final stop. For a while she ignores the knock of this crude intruder, but in time, reality barges in and with it comes despair, hopelessness and many other unwelcome guests.

Is this the end of the road? Is this punishment for past sins? Is there anything to live for? Or could this be the beginning of a journey that can bring this dear woman nearer to the heart of God? How will she know for sure? Who will help her discover the truth?

Praise God! There is another knock at this nursing home resident's door. It is people like those on Lucy's and Doug's teams. They do not arrive with all the right answers, but are willing to take the time to listen, pray, and share a word of hope from the Bible. In the midst of such a union, our God of Love abides. He touches both the hurting resident and the caring visitors. He shines His light and imparts unexplainable blessings that almost always result in eternal treasures. I have seen this kind of event unfold many times, and by God's grace, have had the privilege to assist in building the bridge that unites these hearts.

So if you sense a tug in your heart to care for the people confined in a long term care facility, I believe your tug is from God. I believe He loves these lonely neighbors of ours and wants to show His love through you. I believe that once you take the steps shared in this guidebook, you will agree with us who are also called, that some of the greatest treasures in this world are hidden within the nursing home walls. You will also find that this community of people long for the hope and peace Jesus promised; and that God is using the willing, even the timid and unassuming believers in the back pews, to help fulfill these needs. What an awesome privilege we share in God's plan to bless them!

"Come follow me," Jesus said, "and I will make you fishers of men." Matthew 4:19

The principles I will share are based on many things I have learned since my first nursing home visit in 1984. My goal is not to explain *how to provide ministry in a care center*; rather, I offer a detailed plan for *how and where to get your church started* in this great outreach. There are other excellent resources that can help you understand how to minister in a care facility which I will mention later. My insights are not limited to my own experiences and studies. God has also taught me through the countless people I have met traveling throughout North America to train and network with nursing home missionaries.

For now, let me suggest you first read through this entire guidebook, which I trust will create deep excitement in your heart as well as give you an overall picture of the process you can expect to experience. Then come back to chapter one and take your next steps into what you may find to be an inexpressible and glorious joy.

A few footnotes:

I trust that you will enjoy this guidebook and the labor of love I am going to assist you with. Explaining my language / terminology might make it easier for you to understand and benefit from this guidebook. Below are a few of the terms I use:

- I use the titles nursing homes, care centers, care facilities and long term care facilities interchangeably. Although they can have different meanings in different areas of the country, they all boil down to long term health care campuses that house people with health-related needs.

- For you who are English majors, you will notice I do not use a hyphen when referring to long term care centers. This is a common practice in the health care industry. You may also recognize other imperfections in my writing. *I hope you can excuse me and understand that I started out as a mechanic and not a writer.*

- When referring to people, I use the pronouns: he, she, his, her, etc. interchangeably.

- I will often refer to our book, <u>NURSING HOME MINISTRY - Where Hidden Treasures Are Found</u>. My friend, Dr. Tom McCormick, a nursing home ministry veteran since the 70's, and I have written this book. Now in its third printing, I highly recommend it as a more comprehensive guide to all aspects of nursing home ministry. I will refer to this book as "<u>NURSING HOME MINISTRY</u>".

- I will also refer to our video training curriculum, <u>LIVING WATERS IN A DRY LAND</u>. This eight-session video enables volunteers to benefit from the principles that have been used to train thousands of volunteers in North America. I will refer to this resource as <u>LIVING WATERS</u>.

11

CHAPTER ONE

The mission field

I consider each long term care facility to be a part of an overall **huge** mission field. Though not overseas or on foreign soil, these campuses sustain a people group that have genuine spiritual needs that only the Lord's people can help fulfill. Since the residents of nursing homes are generally confined to their community, caring Christians must be willing to enter into their cultural and governing structures to look for appropriate ways to help them know and love Jesus.

In America, there are over 16,000 nursing homes and 39,000 assisted living facilities, housing more than 2 million residents. As our population ages over the next 25 years, the number of residents and facilities is projected to double. It is also estimated that 1/3 of all Americans who die in the current year will have spent all or part of their last six months in a long term care facility. This is over 800,000 people per year; this number exceeds the population of individual states such as Wyoming, Alaska, Delaware, South Dakota or Vermont. This number exceeds the casualties of any single natural disaster in over 2000 years.

With this in mind, I think it is important for us to ask questions such as:

- Where are the residents going to spend eternity?
- Whose responsibility is it to help them find hope and peace in Christ Jesus?
- Does God really care enough to equip and send forth committed servants to shine His light in this white harvest field?

You Bet!!!

> *Nursing home ministry is a compassionate move inspired by God. He is building His church inside the care centers throughout America. We who have given ourselves to this work are actually joining God in His great plan to care for His people.*

Since there are care centers in almost every community, we do not need to move missionary teams to another country. Nevertheless, we must keep in mind that the people in these *sub-communities* are of no less importance to God than the people in an overseas mission field. We must not neglect our responsibility to recruit, train, equip, and support Care Center Missionaries who will also help fulfill the Great Commission of our Lord Jesus in **Matthew 28:18-20; "Then Jesus came to them and said, "All authority in heaven and on earth has been given to me. Therefore go and make disciples of all nations, baptizing them in the name of the Father and of the Son and of the Holy Spirit, and teaching them to obey everything I have commanded you. And surely I am with you always, to the very end of the age."**

It's doable

The responsibility to help meet the spiritual needs of our 2,000,000 neighbors confined in 55,000 facilities may seem overwhelming. But consider: if each church in America would establish only *one* outreach team and adopt only *one* care facility, the spiritual needs of the residents in every home could be met. The 320,000 churches in our nation can provide the needed spiritual care in our 55,000 care facilities. It is very doable! The primary requirement is a sincere willingness to obey our Lord Jesus. I am deeply grateful for the nearly 20,000 churches who have responded to the Lord by embracing this call. It is my ambition to help the many who have not, to recognize God's Word and respond with humility and zeal. For the One who said, *"Whatever you did for one of the least of these brothers of mine, you did for me,"* has also said, *"Whatever you did not do for one of the least of these, you did not do for me" (Matthew 25:31-46).*

How it's being done

Over the past several years, God Cares Ministry has had the privilege of helping hundreds of churches plant a *spiritual garden* in various care centers. We call these gardens nursing home ministry care teams. A care team is a small group of people committed to work together to share the Love and Word of Jesus through one-to-one visits and/or group worship services and Bible studies. I see each care team as a garden planted in a care facility by the Lord's leading. By the power of His Word and Spirit, the Lord causes each garden to produce much good fruit.

It only takes two people to make a team for one-to-one visiting. For group worship services, a team of four to eight is recommended. A clear overview of a care team and the responsibilities of each member is located in chapter six of the book, NURSING HOME MINISTRY. That book, along with the video training series, LIVING WATERS IN A DRY LAND,

14

have become primary tools to help care teams understand how to provide life-giving ministry in care centers.

God Cares Ministry strives to encourage and support every Christian church in developing a care team who will adopt a nursing home in their own community. We have now grown to over 1,000 people actively volunteering and/or contributing toward our cause. Many of these special servants are using the tools God has led us to develop and continue to experience the joy of helping their friends take Jesus' hand.

If you are serious about bringing the Gospel to folks in care centers, Bill Goodrich has the best tool box of ideas that I know. We have used many of the tools that he teaches to expand our nursing home/care center ministry over the last four years. If you are eager to bring the Good News to these dear people, you will find this guidebook to be excellent for getting started; helping you dive right into this exciting ministry. Through this and other tools from God Cares Ministry, your volunteers will see incredible results as you bring the Love of Jesus to residents.

Mary Courtney, Christ Community Chapel, Aurora, OH

While we are thrilled with this growth, we cannot rest – given that there are still many thousands of unreached people spending their last days in a long term care facility.

It's God's garden – it's our privilege

Simply put, nursing home ministry is not on the average pastor's radar screen. In fact, over 90% of the churches in America do not even have such an outreach on their list of recognized and budgeted ministries. Since this mission field has little visibility in the church, most people have not yet considered the needs of the residents and the opportunity to serve them. For those of you who grieve over such neglect, take heart! Our experience is that in almost every church, the Lord is stirring the hearts of a few people whom He is calling to serve in this specialized work. Remember, our Father in Heaven is very concerned for these lonely friends of His. He loves them personally and He takes the initiative to lead His servants into this *white harvest field*. Since you have been led to purchase this guidebook, it is very likely that you are one of the servants the Lord will use to help develop your church's care team. By His Word and Holy Spirit He will call forth workers for this spiritual garden. In the same manner, He can use you to coordinate the efforts of His workers so that they may know the joy of bearing fruit for God's glory.

We must see ourselves as God's chosen workers. He is the Lord of the Harvest who directs our steps. As Jesus has promised in *John 15:1-8*, when we abide in Him and in His Word, He will have us accomplish the possible while He handles the impossible.

When I think about how the Lord has raised up and sustained God Cares Ministry since 1994, how He has allowed us to develop hundreds of care teams, how He has enabled us to directly and indirectly minister to countless thousands of people He loves, and now the joy of producing resources that are helping to spread His work across America...

then sings my soul, "My God, how great Thou art!"

> *Commit your works to the Lord and*
> *your plans will be established.*
> *Proverbs 16:3*

CHAPTER TWO

First steps

Starting a nursing home ministry care team may seem a bit overwhelming, but really it is not. Good planning, patience and a willingness to take one step at a time, will allow the process to become a joyful journey with the Lord. I plan to cover in detail every step, phase and goal that you will need to consider. *2Chronicles 15:2* states, *"The LORD is with you when you are with him."* Therefore, I recommend the following initial steps be taken as a season of personal preparation.

1. **Pray:** Pray especially for wisdom, understanding, and direction. A season of prayer and fasting has been the practice of many believers who have experienced the Lord's presence in their ministry. Many of us have made unnecessary mistakes because we have not taken the time to pray. If possible, pray with other believers who are currently ministering in a nursing home. *Nehemiah Chapter 1* presents a great example of a season of prayer that not only moved God's heart, but the hearts of many people whom God used in an amazing way.

2. **Study God's Word:** It is important to understand God's perspective if we desire to be effective in any ministry. In our book, NURSING HOME MINISTRY, you will find over 250 Scripture references related to this ministry. A good Bible concordance will assist you in finding many more. Writing out verses that focus on what God says about ministry to the elderly, widows, the sick, the grieving, etc. will help you gain a clear perspective of God's will. Since we see developing a care team as planting a spiritual garden, you will find much encouragement and wisdom in verses that speak of gardening, planting, fruitfulness, and the like. I have

17

given the address to many such verses in this guidebook and highly encourage you to meditate on them during your quiet times with the Lord.

3. **Learn from experienced nursing home missionaries:** There is a wealth of wisdom and insight in the hearts of those who have faithfully served God for the past several years. There may be some in a nearby church or perhaps in your own congregation you can contact, or even serve with for a season. Any time you can arrange to spend with an experienced volunteer in a care center will be extremely valuable! If there are none, you may want to move ahead into "Phase One", which is outlined in chapter three, as part of your preparation.

There is also a great wealth of knowledge shared in books, newsletters, websites, and videos. In addition to the resources produced by God Cares Ministry, I have listed a number of other helpful materials in Appendix A.

4. **Stay focused:** There are many needs and opportunities to do many good works. You may need to refrain from certain opportunities or perhaps wean yourself from other activities. Consider the Kingdom principle in *Matthew 13:44-46.*

It is also a good practice to keep a personal journal for writing out key Scriptures, your prayers and thoughts that you will receive as you seek the Lord. These Words, ideas, and prayers will be helpful in formulating a clear vision *(Habakkuk 2:2).*

5. **Seek to obtain your Pastor's support:** This is not a time for laying out long-term plans. We will do this later. At this point I recommend that you share with your pastor *only* your desire to serve in this kind of ministry under the church's covering. You can also ask him to provide the following support:

> ➢ Pray for you as you seek the Lord's direction regarding this ministry.

➤ Point you to other Scriptures related to serving the elderly or those confined in institutions.

➤ Encourage one other church member to join with you in either ministry or intercessory prayer. A committed friend will be a great source of encouragement and support *(Ecclesiastes 4:9-12)*. He may even know of church members who currently visit in a care facility and would love to have you serve with them.

A humble and submissive spirit will be appreciated and will often win the favor of your pastor.

The above efforts are very important and are in keeping with the A.S.K. principles in *Matthew 7:7-8.*

Ask and it will be given to you; Seek and you will find; Knock and the door will be open to you. For everyone who Asks receives; he who Seeks finds; and to him who Knocks, the door will be opened.

Do not be in a hurry to accomplish the above steps. This is not an idle time, it is an active time of wise preparation *(Proverbs 19:2, Matthew 7:24-25).* Four to ten weeks is a reasonable season for a facilitator or leader to walk through this stage.

As you, and hopefully your friend, accomplish the above steps you will gain insight to these key elements:

- A clear sense of God's will regarding you and this mission field
- Some practical experience from other experienced visitors
- A glimpse of the treasures that are hidden inside the care centers

Check list:

☐ I have prayed for God's leading and wisdom
☐ I have studied God's Word regarding this ministry

19

- ☐ I have sought out the advice of experienced nursing home missionaries
- ☐ I am adjusting my schedule to make time and stay focused in this ministry
- ☐ I have met with my pastor to seek his affirmation and support

Foundational Scriptures to study:

Matthew 28:18-20	*Acts 1:8*
Proverbs 19:2	*Matthew 25:31-46*
Ecclesiastes 4:9-12	*Matthew 9:36-38*
Philippians 4:13	*Matthew 13:1-46*
Proverbs 16:3	*Nehemiah 1:1-11*

One Blessing After Another

The most amazing thing about visiting in nursing homes is the greatness of God's blessing that falls on us and the people we visit at the same time. God has given us the wisdom and privilege to do His will as found in **Matthew 25:40**. *When the dear people thank us and say "God bless you", it is God's love that we feel. It is* **so** *amazing how both we and the residents experience His love at the same time. It never fails! His gift of love to us is the most important thing that happens.*

No matter how busy we are with daily living, when we take the time to visit those who are confined, God's great blessing compensates 100 times over for it! We soon learn that we need the people who live there as much as they need us.

The testimony of faith, alive in bodies and minds that are failing and frail, encourages us and strengthens us even more than most sermons, because we see it alive and active every time we go. Come and see!!! Mary Ann Goodrich

20

Notes: _____

Notes: _____

_____

_____

_____

_____

_____

_____

_____

_____

_____

_____

_____

_____

_____

_____

_____

_____

_____

_____

_____

_____

_____

_____

_____

_____

CHAPTER THREE

Seven Phases

Once you have taken your five steps of preparation (as shown in chapter two) you've laid the firm foundation needed for an enduring ministry. Now you are ready to begin what I call the Seven-Phase Process. In summary, the seven phases are as follows:

Phase one: Choose the location where you will plant

> Decide on a care center and develop a rapport and suitable plan with the staff

Phase two: Obtain permission and guidelines to plant

> Connect with your church's vision and leadership

Phase three: Gathering the right seed and plants

> Recruiting church members for a care team

Phase four: Planting the seeds and plants

> Your first few visits

Phase five: Nurturing the plants

> Educating your care team

Phase six: Protecting and supporting the plants

> Encouraging and supporting your care team

Phase seven: Enjoying the fruit

> That you might know the joy of Jesus

Now, let's take a closer look at each phase and how to accomplish it. You will notice that under each phase there are a few goals for completing it.

> *Your circumstances may warrant skipping one or more of these goals but please be sure you understand the intent and take no short cuts. Seventeen years of helping develop care teams has proven to me over and over that there **are** no short cuts. Adjustments and tweaking are often needed; yet the teams I have helped develop, that are experiencing desired fruitfulness, are the ones who were willing to go through the phases without compromise.*

You will also notice that under most phases there are **"Possible hurdles"** comments and **"Extra mile tips**.**"** These are:

Possible hurdles: These are possible concerns or challenges you may encounter while trying to accomplish the goals of a particular phase. With the hurdles, I will give you a few suggestions to overcome them. These suggestions along with prayer and your creativity should keep you moving forward.

Extra mile tips: It is my experience that long term success comes not only to the one who prays and has integrity, but also to the few who are willing to go the extra mile or invest a few extra hours. Doing the little extra things will make a lot of difference, for example: spending an extra portion of time to do something right, clarifying communication, adding a personal touch to a project, a thank you note, etc. These extra mile efforts are not always necessary, but when humbly given in love, they can yield much fruitfulness.

PHASE ONE:

Choose the location where you will plant

The first step in planting a garden is to find the right setting. Proper sunlight, watering and a hedge of protection are important factors. The great thing about your spiritual garden is that your team members are followers of Jesus. Christians already have the Sonshine, Living Water, and the power of Jesus' Name to protect them. The concern is, will the care center desire and support this garden? My experience is that almost every nursing home desires the fruit of the Spirit, but we must approach it with wisdom.

> ***Peacemakers who sow in peace raise a harvest of righteousness.*** *James 3:18*

Phase One Goals:

    #1 – Decide on a nursing home
    #2 – Meet with nursing home staff and develop a plan
    #3 – Get established in the home
    #4 – Enjoy yourself

Goal #1   Decide on a nursing home

Sometimes a church will look for a nursing home in their community and find that there are several within a twenty-minute drive. Wanting to have the most impact, they choose to divide their time between four or five homes, visiting each home once a month, on a rotating basis. Although this may sound like a good idea, I highly recommend that you choose **only one** home that is near your church. There are a number of reasons for this:

- Weekly visits in one home enable you to establish deeper relationships with residents, staff, and families. The better you know your new friends, the more you will understand their needs and how to help them.

- Teams that rotate through several care centers on a monthly basis take more effort to organize and maintain.

- The closer the nursing home is to the church, the more accessible it will be for most church members.

- After you are well established and effectively ministering in the home, your church's faithfulness will be a clear testimony to the nursing home community *(John 13:35).*

- The closer your church is to the nursing home, the more accessible it will be for staff, residents' families and sometimes even residents who may want to attend.

For these reasons, I recommend that your team focus on only one nursing home in your church's community, and that you make it your goal to visit on a weekly basis. If the team grows to eight or more consistent team members, a second team could be established to adopt a second nursing home in the community. This team should function independently but the two teams should come together periodically for fellowship, encouragement and prayer support.

> *I do not want to give the impression that once-a-month visits in several homes are improper. They can be a great blessing. But please keep the above points in mind while planning your outreach.*

Goal #2   Meet with the nursing home staff

The next goal is to meet with the appropriate nursing home staff. The Activities Director of the nursing home will be your primary connection. She is the person with whom you want to make an appointment to share your desires. If the home has a Chaplain or Volunteer Coordinator, you may be directed to one of them.

Let the Activities Director know of your desire to visit residents who have few or no visitors. Additionally, share your hope to establish an outreach group from your church who visit, and perhaps conduct worship services or Bible studies if appropriate.

Extra mile tip: Since you do not yet have a ministry care team formed, I recommend that you begin by making personal and ongoing visits with residents while you continue through the next few phases. This will familiarize you with the care center environment and allow you to establish a rapport with key staff members. When your care team begins their visits (in phase four) you will already be comfortable and better able to focus on the team members' needs in this new environment.

Possible hurdle: Nursing homes are normally in great need of volunteers and will welcome your church's participation. If there is any hesitation from the Activities Director, it is likely related to a concern that you would be proselytizing. If this concern is raised, you need to be able to truthfully explain that your purpose is not to try to change people's religion; that you simply desire to make friendly visits and perhaps read the Bible and pray with ones who desire it. The reasons for this are clearly spelled out in the first chapters of NURSING HOME MINISTRY.

The Activities Director will want to know what church you represent, your Pastor's name, and contact information. She may have you fill out a Volunteer's Registration Form, and some facilities may even require a background check and a tuberculosis (TB) test. Though the latter is rare, it is done to safeguard the residents and you will need to comply.

Understanding the expectations and needs of the Activities Director and also communicating your hopes for your church to adopt this home, makes for great bridge-building! I recommend your discussion includes the following points:

- What days and times are best for one-to-one visits
- Is there a need for a worship service or Bible study
- What days and times are best for a group activity
- You plan on training your team. Would she like to participate (I will give more detail on this in phase four)

Use the "Notes" pages in this guidebook to write out your agreed-upon schedules and plans.

The Activities Director will work out a mutually agreeable schedule for your initial visits and also develop a tentative plan in anticipation of more volunteers coming. Next, she will take you on a tour of the facility and introduce you to a few residents. She will likely introduce you, also, to key staff people. This is helpful for establishing an accepted presence, as the staff needs to know you are an official volunteer.

> *Don't be apprehensive about this meeting. You can be fairly certain that the Activities Director is excited about finding trustworthy volunteers to help with activities and personal visits.*

Possible hurdle: On rare occasions, an Activities Director may not be willing to support your desires or be open to having your church make regular visits. Over the years, I have had this happen only a few times. Instead of forcing my way into the home, I visit other nursing homes in the area to discern where the Lord is leading. Discerning spiritual hunger among the residents and a supportive Activities Director are good signs of good soil for the garden.

Goal #3   Get established in the home

Getting well established is merely a matter of following through on the decisions you made with the Activities Director. NURSING HOME MINISTRY provides several tips for establishing a welcome presence in the care center. If you should encounter an unforeseen problem, be sure to seek direction from the Activities Director or appropriate staff.

Goal #4   Enjoy yourself

It is easy to get overly focused on the process and goals of your ministry. Remember, there are many wonderful people to meet who can become your treasured friends. Learn to be fully present with each person you have the opportunity to meet *(by focusing only on that person and not on other things)*. The fruit of love is joy *(John 15:9-13)*, and your joy in the Lord will be contagious!

Check list:

- ☐ I have decided on an appropriate care center
- ☐ I have met with the Activities Director
- ☐ I have a visiting schedule and list of people to visit
- ☐ I have a general understanding of the volunteer responsibilities
- ☐ I understand some of the practical and spiritual needs that my church can help meet at this care center
- ☐ I have the above items written in my ministry journal
- ☐ I have begun personal visits with a few residents
- ☐ I am enjoying my visits at the care center

Phase one Scriptures to study:

Proverbs 3:1-35	*Philippians 4:4-9*
James 1:27	*Isaiah 58:6-12*
John 13:34-35	*Joshua 1:6-9*
John 15:1-17	*Romans 13:1-5*
Matthew 7:24-25	

Notes: _____

_____

_____

_____

_____

_____

_____

_____

_____

_____

_____

_____

_____

_____

_____

_____

_____

_____

_____

_____

_____

_____

Notes: _____

_____

_____

_____

_____

_____

_____

_____

_____

_____

_____

_____

_____

_____

_____

_____

_____

_____

_____

_____

_____

_____

_____

_____

_____

_____

_____

PHASE TWO:

Obtain permission and guidelines to plant

Keep in mind that in this gardening process, you are planting Christian volunteers from your church group who will ultimately be bearing fruit in the care facility. I trust God will give you some "plants" from the back pews who have not yet experienced the privilege of serving in a ministry. You will find that some are just waiting to be asked to help and serve within an organized plan.

There is often a proper procedure by which your church handles ministry launching. Your potential volunteers currently have a "gardener" (the pastor and church leaders) who want to assure that the plants are ready for such a responsibility, and that you will provide appropriate facilitation.

Obey your leaders and submit to their authority. They keep watch over you as men who must give an account. Obey them so that their work will be a joy, not a burden, for that would be of no advantage to you. Hebrews 13:17

Phase Two Goals:

 #1 – Prepare to meet with your Pastor
 #2 – Meet with your Pastor
 #3 – Write down the plan

If you are going to develop a care team within your church, you must have your pastor's support. Generally, this is an easy task because pastors want to see church members actively growing in their faith. He will very likely support all your efforts if he sees that you will conduct yourself in a manner worthy of the gospel of Christ - as you represent Him and your church in this mission field *(Philippians 1:27)*.

Goal #1   Prepare to meet with your pastor

You have already completed 90% of this goal because you have taken the time to follow the steps in the previous pages. Congratulations! All of these steps and goals have worked together to reveal the great mission field that is right in your own community. As Jesus said, it is *"White for the harvest" John 4:35.*

Your first meeting with your pastor (step 5 in chapter 2) was primarily to share your burden for the people in care centers and to obtain his support as you sought the Lord's will and guidance. This next meeting will give you an opportunity to share what you have learned during this season and what you sense is the next step for planting the garden. To complete this goal, I recommend you consider the following points:

- Think of the general procedures which your church follows to start an outreach. Be sure to take these into consideration and have a general plan to respectfully follow the protocol.

- How would your nursing home outreach fit into the vision of the church? Most churches have within their vision statement a goal to share God's love in the community. This, of course, is an easy fit for your vision.

- Consider the questions your pastor is likely to ask to help him understand your overall vision and plan. Below are some of the common questions he may ask. Be prepared to share answers to these with a servant-like attitude *(Nehemiah 2:1-8).*

  1. What are the needs of the residents at the nursing home?
  2. What do you think you and your church can do to help meet these needs?
  3. Is meeting these needs something the Lord wants your church to do?
  4. How does this opportunity fit in with your church's vision/mission?
  5. What resources will you need?

Extra mile tip: You may want to talk with other mature believers who will listen to and even challenge (but not discourage) your ideas. This process will help you consider other aspects of your proposal and help you polish your communication skills. This is a common practice of mine and has helped me develop short, concise answers that are better received than my sometimes overly long and detailed explanations.

Goal #2   Meet with your pastor

Now that you have prepared yourself for meeting your pastor, it is time to make the appointment. It is best to call the church during the week to make a one-hour appointment. Please do not try to arrange this meeting on Sunday between services. He will appreciate not having to consider other issues that might distract from those present responsibilities and needs of the congregation.

> According to *Ephesians 4:11-12*, Pastors are responsible to initiate or facilitate, but not necessarily operate, ministries of helps like nursing home outreach. This meeting will help your pastor discern if nursing home ministry is something the Lord wants your church to embrace. He has the responsibility to make such decisions and to weave appropriate ministries into the church's fabric. Don't be anxious or try to *sell* your ideas. The Lord loves the residents and your church. He knows what a blessing awaits those who obey His call to love our neighbors. Your job is to do the possible (respectfully communicate). God's job is to do the impossible (move the hearts of people into His will).

There are three objectives to this meeting. If you accomplish these, you will not only have answered most of your pastor's questions, you will also have obtained his favor and direction to press on through phase three. Let's outline each objective:

A. **Give a brief overview** of what you have been doing and learning as you have walked through the goals of phase one. Be sure to include one of the primary Scripture verses that has compelled you to this point.

34

B. **Explain your desire** to establish a nursing home ministry care team to adopt the care center.

   1. He will need to know what a care team is and what is required of each team member. See appendix B for a brief description. You are welcome to copy and modify if necessary.

   2. Be ready to share how you sense a nursing home outreach fits into your church's vision/mission.

   3. Be sure your pastor understands that you and the team are willing to do the actual work of the ministry, but welcome him to participate as often as he may desire. Some pastors really enjoy and have a special gift for nursing home ministry and may want to be involved on a regular basis, but usually he will want to delegate the responsibility to you and your care team.

C. **Ask for support and input** to accomplish phases 3, 4 and 5: recruiting team members, planting and nurturing the care team.

   1. Ask for an opportunity to present the ministry to the congregation, preferably during a Sunday morning service. Details for this will be shared in Phase three.

   2. Consider an appropriate time to walk the team through an orientation and a training program. Details for this will be shared in Phases four and five.

   3. It is not expected that your pastor lead these, but it is essential that the church sees his earnest support of this outreach. Therefore, I recommend you ask him to be present during your church presentation, the team's orientation in the nursing home, and at the opening of the training program. This kind of pastoral support will be most helpful and encouraging to all whom the Lord is calling into this mission field.

   4. Be prepared to present a "Ministry start-up budget." Unless you are planning to cover the *minor* expenses,

your pastor will need to know your probable financial needs.

5. Be sure to listen carefully to your pastor's comments and express gratitude for his support and leadership. You may want to offer him a copy of this Guidebook so he has a clear understanding of what you are hoping to accomplish.

Finally, do not stretch the meeting past the scheduled time. If there are details that still need to be shared, you can summarize them in a follow-up letter or meeting. Before you leave (if he has not already offered) ask your pastor to conclude this meeting by praying for you and the birth of this new outreach.

Goal #3   Write it down

Clear communication is a beautiful thing. Many problems arise when we think and act on something we thought the other person said, only later to find he meant something different. One way to be sure of clear communication with your pastor and other leaders is to write down what you believe was agreed upon during your meeting, and then submit this to your pastor for review and affirmation. Be sure to include a listing of the decided goals, who is responsible to achieve them, and the date you plan to have these accomplished.

This letter should reveal a submissive spirit and could state, "I am so grateful for your support and commitment to the development of this new nursing home ministry outreach. I have summarized the details of what we decided during our meeting. Please let me know if this is accurate and complete. Thank you for all you are doing to build up the Kingdom of God."

Possible hurdle: The pastor may be concerned that you are taking on more than you are capable of handling. Your pastor may recommend you set some limitations. Be submissive and faithful and *"Don't despise the day of small things" (Zechariah 4:10).*

36

As you remain humble and committed, you will have many more open doors. The prayer of Nehemiah is an especially relevant one before you speak with your pastor or other church leaders:

O Lord, let your ear be attentive to the prayer of this your servant and to the prayer of your servants who delight in revering your name. Give your servant success today by granting him favor in the presence of this man. Nehemiah 1:11

Check list:

- ☐ I have prayerfully thought through my meeting with my pastor
- ☐ I have shared my ideas with another mature believer who has helped me prepare for my meeting and future plans
- ☐ I have reached my three objectives during the meeting with my pastor
- ☐ I have sent the pastor a follow-up letter to affirm plans for the next phases
- ☐ I have recorded these objectives in my ministry journal

Phase two Scriptures to study:

Habakkuk 2:2	*Zechariah 4:10*
Nehemiah 1:11 & 2:1-8	*John 4:35*
Ephesians 4:11-12	*Philippians 1:27*

Jesus said, "Whoever serves me must follow me; and where I am my servant also will be. My Father will honor the one who serves me." (John 12:26)

Before you begin phase Three, I would like to pause and tell you how excited I am that you are taking these steps of faith. You are breaking ground for developing a ministry that honors our Heavenly Father. You can never realize on Earth the countless numbers of people and the full benefits they will obtain through your sacrifices of love. Yet, we will all enjoy them in heaven, for all eternity. May our King Jesus continually bless you with his peace and joy as you follow Him.

A Gift for you

If you have been able to check off all the items on your check lists from pages 19, 20, 29, and 37, you deserve applause for your achievements!!! You are now eligible to contact God Cares Ministry to add your ministry to our ever-growing list of ministry friends. We will:

- Add you and your ministry to our prayer list.
- Send you our inspirational and informational newsletter.
- Send you a free video to assist you in the next phase.

Of course, if you already have a ministry team up and running, you are welcome to sign-up as well. Also, we will not share your contact information with a third party.

There are several ways for you to add your ministry:

- Send in the postcard that came with this book.
- Use our website www.GodCaresMinistry.com and click on add my ministry.
- Send an email to info@GodCaresMinistry.com.
- Call our office during regular business hours: 440-930-2173. If you call, we will pray for you over the phone.

Notes: _____

_____

_____

_____

_____

_____

_____

_____

_____

_____

_____

_____

_____

_____

_____

_____

_____

_____

_____

_____

_____

_____

_____

_____

_____

_____

_____

_____

PHASE THREE:

Gathering the right seed and plants

There are two kinds of volunteers for your care team: 1) New Christians who are just learning to love and follow Jesus; they are like seeds ready for soil, and 2) Growing Christians who have been abiding in Christ; they are like plants, ready to bear fruit when placed in the right environment. It is likely that the Lord will send both seeds and plants to your garden. As you keep the ministry focused on Jesus' love and His Word, He will create unity and fruitfulness through all His servants.

Jesus said, "He who abides in Me, and I in him, bears much fruit; for without Me you can do nothing." (see John 15:5)

Phase Three Goals:

#1 – Be prepared
#2 – Present the opportunity to the congregation
#3 – Follow-up

Now that you have your pastor's support, your next step will be to recruit church members for your care team. Remember, when recruiting help, you are asking people to give one of life's most valued resources – TIME. Volunteers need to sense that there is an immediate and important need and a specific plan to meet that need. Proper preparation, presentation, and follow-up are essential. That's why I am going to share a lot of good ideas to help you. As mentioned earlier, you do not have to do everything I say. Your circumstances may warrant some innovation and modification, or even skipping one of my suggested tasks, but make sure you understand the intent and take no short cuts. Every phase will walk you through helpful exercises and experiences that will serve you in developing important skills and a fruitful ministry.

Goal #1   Be prepared

You will need to prepare to give your church a clear, concise overview of the primary needs of the people in the nursing home, and the opportunity to be used by God to meet these needs. Your pastor will help you decide when the best date is for you to share; and you want to make sure it is put on the church calendar. He will also give you a specific amount of time to share. Please do not take more time than given. He will appreciate your submissiveness!

You will need to create a signup sheet to obtain the name, phone number, and email address of those who express interest. It is helpful to ask if they have specific days/evenings available. This sheet could be included in the church bulletin so they can drop it in the offering basket. There is much value in having a informational table with pictures and nursing home ministry resources that can be previewed or even borrowed. You can include a tray of cookies or some snacks to encourage a visit from people like me ☺.

At the same time you are preparing your presentation, you will also need to be arranging an initial orientation visit for those who will sign up. This is a casual, get-acquainted time for your volunteers and the residents. I will give you details about this in phase four. But for now, you will need to arrange this important gathering with the Activities Director who will work out the best time and details with you.

Goal #2   Present the opportunity to the congregation

Having this orientation arranged before you present the ministry to your church is important because it will allow you to keep the process moving forward. Too many times the desire of those who sign up fizzles down if they are not soon engaged. Therefore I recommend you try to have them in the nursing home within two weeks of the time they sign up. Once they are in the home, desire will be nurtured by the residents and God's Spirit.

Your presentation should be upbeat, Biblically based, and encouraging. Focus primarily on the positive blessings you have experienced during your past several visits. To help you consider sharing points for a five-minute presentation, I have provided an example of what could be included:

- Good morning!
- A few months ago, I began to visit nursing home name.
- At first, I was afraid because _____.
- After a few visits (share your experience)
- I realized how lonely and spiritually hungry these people are.
- In **John 4:35, Jesus said, "Do you not say, 'Four months more and then the harvest'? I tell you, open your eyes and look at the fields! They are ripe for harvest."** I see this nursing home as a mission field that is ripe for harvest!
- Nursing home residents have the same needs as all of us. One primary need is for Christian fellowship that will help them to find hope and peace in Jesus.
- The problem is that they are not able to leave the nursing home to attend a church of their choice.
- It has been my prayer that the Lord would enable our church to establish a ministry to visit and help these folks.
- We can "adopt" this home and provide fellowship and spiritual refreshment.
- Some of you may be asking the Lord about the kind of ministry He would have you serve. This is a mission field where individuals, families or small groups can really make an eternal difference in people's hearts.
- Jesus said in **Matthew 25:40, "I tell you the truth, whatever you did for one of the least of these brothers of mine, you did for me."** In verses 35 and 36 Jesus said, **"For I was hungry and you gave me something to eat, I was thirsty and you gave me something to drink, I was a stranger and you invited me in, I needed clothes and you**

clothed me, I was sick and you looked after me, I was in prison and you came to visit me. "

- The Bible also says in *James 1:27, "Religion that God our Father accepts as pure and faultless is this: to look after orphans and widows in their distress..."*

- I am grateful that Pastor _____ supports this ministry and how it helps fulfill our church's vision to:_____ (here you can quote the portion of your church's vision that would include ministry to nursing homes).

- God has touched my heart over these past months by ___ (here, you can share a brief testimony of a recent blessing you experienced).

- I have arranged with the nursing home staff for our church to bring refreshments for an informal gathering to meet some of the residents. This time will start with a half-hour video and a brief time of prayer before we meet the residents.

- In a few months we will be providing ministry training to develop our church's ministry team for those who desire to continue visits.

- The residents and staff at the nursing home desire our visits. The Door is Wide Open!

- You are welcome to purchase or you may borrow my NURSING HOME MINISTRY book for a glimpse of this great ministry. It will help you realize that this is a viable mission field right in our community!

- I have come today to speak on behalf of those who cannot speak for themselves. Come and see how you can be used of the Lord to give Him a drink through very thirsty people in our community.

- I will be at the ministry table after the service to talk further with you and give you a handout with more details.

- May the Lord bless and guide you in your decisions.

You can see from the above example that there are three main points:

1. There is a great need.
2. There is a specific plan to meet the need.
3. Any Christian who wants to serve the Lord can be part of an outreach that will help meet the need.

Whether you use this example or develop your own, you need to clearly address these three points and one or two pertinent Scriptures to validate your overall message. If you can write your own outline and share it with your prayer partner, it will help you develop a passionate, concise, and heart-felt presentation.

I have given many such presentations and sometimes feel like I could have done a better job, yet I am always encouraged *and amazed* at how the Lord sends interested people. I have come to realize that the Lord has already been tugging at the hearts of some in the congregation. They want to serve Him but are waiting for a sign or the invitation. Be confident that the Lord of the Harvest has heard your prayers to send forth the workers for the harvest *(Matthew 9:36-38).*

Extra mile tip: You will not be able to give all the details in your short presentation. However, sharing full details in a brief handout will increase your communication effectiveness. Be sure to include your contact information, as some will want to pray and perhaps call you with questions before they make their decision.

Possible hurdle: Avoid over packing your evening before the presentation with responsibility. Late busy evenings and rushed mornings can be tiring and distracting. Conversely, a relaxing morning that includes quiet time and prayer support with a mature believer will increase your confidence and brighten your smile.

By this time, you should have added your ministry to our list of ministry friends, if so, you will be receiving a DVD with a few recruiting videos that can help. "Wait!" some of you will say, "You mean all this is in a video, and I don't have to terrify myself by standing in front of an audience? Why didn't you just tell me

44

and avoid raising my blood pressure?" To be honest with you, I am really excited about this video, and would love to have it shared in every church; but I also know the value of your passionate presentation. I believe the Lord will best use both you *and* the video together to encourage His servants to step out in faith.

Possible Hurdle: Large churches that have multiple services on Sunday morning will not always afford time for a presentation. For this and other reasons, your pastor may not permit a presentation to be given to the whole church. However, arrangements could be made for you to share with a Sunday school class or some of the church's smaller fellowship groups. Another alternative could be to have your pastor make an announcement about the nursing home ministry for a few consecutive weeks, inviting members to an informational after-service luncheon/discussion. Be sure to include details about this meeting in the church bulletin.

Goal #3   Follow-up

Your willingness to follow up on potential team members is very important. Many people will be touched by a good presentation and may want to try the ministry. However, they may have concerns that need to be addressed. Some of the possible concerns include:

- Fear of getting into an awkward situation with a resident and not knowing what to do
- Fears that they might say or do the wrong thing
- Feeling that they have no special talents and therefore have nothing to give
- Fear of over-committing themselves

Some people may not even be able to verbalize these concerns, but if we are good listeners, we will be able to pick up on some of these fears and feelings of inadequacy. Remind them that the first few visits are for getting acquainted with residents who desire visits. Assure them that there will be training forthcoming, and you will also help them.

Warning: our enemy, the devil, whispers words of doubt and fear to try to stop all of us. However, grace, truth, mutual encouragement, and prayer will overpower him. My experience with such cautious servants is that once they get over the initial concerns, they blossom and flourish. I was very shy and timid when I started over 26 years ago. Had I walked by feeling and not by faith you would not be reading this book!

According to *1Corinthians 12:4-27* and *Romans 12:3-8,* every Christian has at least one gift to share for the common good of others. Some people may not be able to go to the nursing home but would be willing to give administrative help, provide transportation, or childcare. Try to creatively involve every willing servant.

Although you want many team members, the Lord may provide only one. Consider the value of one faithful team member. Paul said of Timothy, *"I have no one else like him, who takes a genuine interest in your welfare. For everyone looks out for his own interests, not those of Jesus Christ. But you know that Timothy has proved himself, because as a son with his father he has served with me in the work of the gospel" (Philippians 2:20-22).* Be faithful and grateful with small beginnings; the Lord will give you many more opportunities for service in the future.

As you go forth to recruit team members, you need not be shy. You are inviting people to participate with our Heavenly Father in a great mission field. As you have been blessed in this ministry, those who accept the invitation will most likely be blessed. Indeed, you are inviting them to invest into heavenly treasures, which last forever.

Check list:

- ☐ I have contacted God Cares Ministry for prayer and support (See page 38)
- ☐ I have a date on the church calendar for my presentation
- ☐ I have prayerfully prepared my presentation
- ☐ I have shared my presentation with my prayer partner and welcomed input for improvements
- ☐ I have arranged an orientation date and plan with the Activities Director
- ☐ I have created an informational handout with details of the next steps for the ministry team
- ☐ I have prepared a sign-up sheet and a table for sharing information and answering questions

Phase three Scriptures to study:

John 4:1-42	*1Corinthians 12:1-31*
Romans 12:1-8	*Matthew 18:19-20*
Matthew 9:35-38	*Isaiah 41:10*
Philippians 2:20-22	*Hebrews 13:5$_b$-6*
Romans 10:8-15	

Notes: _____

_____

_____

_____

_____

_____

_____

_____

_____

_____

_____

_____

_____

_____

_____

_____

_____

_____

_____

_____

_____

_____

_____

_____

_____

Notes: _____

_____

_____

_____

_____

_____

_____

_____

_____

_____

_____

_____

_____

_____

_____

_____

_____

_____

_____

_____

_____

_____

_____

_____

_____

PHASE FOUR:

Planting the seeds and plants

There is one thing I know about gardening that applies here. When you are going to plant a seed or a growing plant, you need plenty of water. In spiritual gardening, prayer is the best water. In previous phases you have prepared the soil. Now in this fourth phase you are going to plant volunteers in God's garden. Be sure you water with plenty of prayer so that each seed and plant takes root. I also recommend a dash of fertilizer which at this time would be gentle reminders about dates, times, apparel, etc, for those who tend to forget.

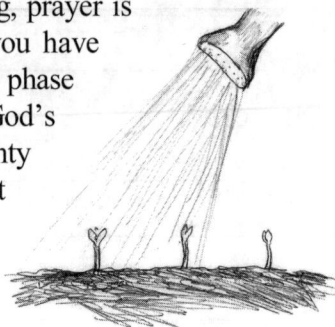

Do not be anxious about anything, but in everything, by prayer and petition, with thanksgiving, present your requests to God. And the peace of God, which transcends all understanding, will guard your hearts and your minds in Christ Jesus. (Philippians 4:6-7)

Goal #1 – Invite volunteers to the orientation
Goal #2 – Facilitate an orientation and first visit
Goal #3 – Follow-up

It is my experience that most volunteers do much better when their first visits do not require spiritual ministry. Many do not know what to say, how they might handle difficult questions or how to lead a resident to Jesus. Some are too aggressive and create unnecessary problems. This is why I recommend that the first several visits are casual, friendly, get acquainted visits. This concern is important and clearly spelled out in chapters 3, 4 & 9 of NURSING HOME MINISTRY which includes a very helpful section called "What to say when you don't know what to say". I also review these principles in the LIVING WATERS training video.

Goal #1 – Invite volunteers to the orientation

As mentioned earlier, on page 41, it is helpful to arrange with the Activities Director an informal social gathering with residents. This will be your team's first introduction to the home and the people who live and work there. It is actually a fun time which minimizes the anxieties of the timid volunteer. I recommend that you ask the team to bring cookies, drinks, and background music in accordance with Activities Director's recommendations. Although you have already told the people about this gathering during your initial communication, and trust me on this one, a friendly reminder with details is necessary.

Goal #2 – Facilitating the orientation and first visit

Before your team actually meets the residents, they should gather in a separate room for a brief introduction to the nursing home; its policies, culture, and volunteer guidelines. The Activities Director will provide some of this and I highly recommend the use of The Sonshine Society's video, "Reaping the Harvest" – particularly, the (first half) of part one. We provide this excerpt in the LIVING WATERS training curriculum. This portion of video will give a great overview and also lots of helpful encouragement for beginning friendships with the residents.

Your agenda for this orientation gathering can be as follows:

10 min. -	Introduce volunteers and Activities Director
15 min. -	Show the short video giving an overview of nursing home ministry
10 min. -	Have the Activities Director give any final comments
5 min. -	Lead the group in prayer
50 min. -	Go to the room where residents will be anticipating your visit and enjoy a wonderful time of fellowship!
15 min. -	Re-gather with volunteers for follow-up questions, encouragement and prayer

This casual time for getting acquainted with residents and the nursing home environment really helps break the ice for timid volunteers. Some groups prefer to have the video viewing at their church and then ride together to the nursing home. Again, please make sure the volunteers realize that the goal is not to provide spiritual ministry at this time, but to just allow the team to get to know the residents. Your next several visits will mostly be with individual residents you met during this gathering. After a few weeks of "friendly visits", your team will have a growing root system. You will then be ready to enter Phase five where I will help you provide training for nurturing the plants for eternal fruit.

Goal #3 – Follow-up

At the end of each of the first several visits, I find it very helpful to gather the team together for a brief time of discussion. I ask them how their experience was and give them the opportunity to share their joys or concerns. This, along with a prayer of thanksgiving puts sensitive closure on concerns as well as increasing the desire to return.

Possible hurdle: On rare occasions, a volunteer has an unpleasant experience that he does not share during the follow-up times. Such thistles could potentially discourage him from returning. When I sense this, I call that person within a day or two explaining I discerned he was struggling with something. Most of the time, your humble encouragement and prayer will get him back on track.

Extra mile tip: It will be a great help to send your pastor a brief letter explaining how things went. He will be encouraged to hear what God is doing. Pastors always appreciate gratitude and some good news!

I was extremely nervous the first time I walked into the nursing home to begin our church ministry. We had met as a care team for months, praying for and planning the ministry and the first steps we would take to get it started. Theoretically, it sounded great! But when it came time to actually step foot in the facility, I was terrified! How do I talk and relate to the residents? Will they hear and understand me? Is this ministry going to make a difference in their lives? Will I say the right thing? These are just a few of the many questions and fears I had. I remember thinking, "Lord..., are you sure this ministry is for me?!?"

He answered me with a big, "YES!" I can honestly say that I have never felt my service fall more in line with God's will than when I am within the walls of the nursing home I was once so timid to enter. Even from that very first visit, it has been so evident that it is God's power, not mine, that touches the souls there. When I give a resident a hug or pat on the shoulder, it is Christ's touch through me. It doesn't matter what words I say as I stand in front of the room full of residents, how awkward I might sound in my opening prayer, or how out of tune my voice is as I lead worship, because it is the power behind the words and the Spirit of God that is working there. I have been on overseas missions for months at a time, yet never have I felt God's presence as I do when I am serving in the nursing home.

Erin Hubbard, Providence Church, Avon, Ohio

Check list:

- ☐ I have been praying for the new volunteers
- ☐ I have sent out a friendly reminder of expectations regarding the orientation
- ☐ I have purchased the orientation video and/or reviewed with Activities Director what will be shared and expected during the orientation
- ☐ I have followed up on possible concerns or issues
- ☐ I have sent my pastor a brief update letter

Phase four Scriptures to study:

John 15:9-17		*1Corinthians 9:19-23*
Proverbs 19:2	*Hebrews 10:23-25*	*James 5:16ᵦ*

53

Notes: _____

_____

_____

_____

_____

_____

_____

_____

_____

_____

_____

_____

_____

_____

_____

_____

_____

_____

_____

_____

_____

_____

_____

_____

PHASE FIVE:

Nurturing the plants

After a few weeks of friendly visits, your seeds will be sprouting and your plants will be hungry for fertilizer. Fertilizer helps us grow and flourish. One such fertilizer is training in Biblical principles for each person's life and for nursing home ministry. I have been greatly encouraged by the many, many comments we receive from those who have attended our training programs. I frequently hear comments like, "I wish I had received this instruction years ago." or "The principles taught in this seminar are not only for nursing home ministry, they apply to all areas of life." and "You have given me a whole new perspective on this ministry."

Do your best to present yourself to God as one approved, a workman who does not need to be ashamed and who correctly handles the word of truth. 2Timothy 2:15

Goal # 1 Decide how you will train

Goal # 2 Provide the training

Goal #3 Apply the principles you were taught

Goal # 1   Decide how you will train

There are a number of avenues for training your team. Not all plants receive the same kind of fertilization and not all volunteers will learn from the same methods of teaching. Therefore, I recommend that you maintain an ongoing opportunity for learning that includes different styles of teaching. The following are a few approaches to consider.

Seminars

Seminars give an overview of many aspects of nursing home ministry. I recommend your team attends at least one of our LIVING WATERS IN A DRY LAND seminars, through our video training curriculum or a live presentation. You will find a preview of this training program on the DVD you received with this book. You will also find lots of helpful information about training on our website, www.GodCaresMinistry.com.

The seminar covers five primary areas:

- The needs and the call to nursing home ministry
- Understanding the spiritual needs of nursing home residents and how they are fulfilled
- One-to-one visitation – How to lead your friend to Jesus
- Group services – How to prepare and share a life-giving devotional
- Ministering to people who have dementia

The Sonshine Society has a basic video called, REAPING THE HARVEST that covers helpful principles for one-to-one visits and group ministry in a nursing home setting. It was produced particularly for beginners and, as mentioned earlier, we use a portion of it during the orientation. In addition to these videos, try to include some role-playing so that volunteers can participate in simulated situations similar to those they may actually encounter.

Books

Written thoughts have great power because they can be read many times over and studied individually and in groups. There are a number of books that focus specifically on nursing home ministry. Of course, my favorite is *NURSING HOME MINISTRY Where Hidden Treasures Are Found*. Dr. Tom McCormick and I have covered most of the issues you will encounter as a nursing home missionary. Some of the topics included are:

- Nursing home ministry in the Bible
- Evangelism in the nursing home

- What to say when you don't know what to say
- How to actively listen
- How to lead a resident to Jesus
- How to prepare and share a life-giving devotional/Bible study
- Suggested models for worship services and Bible studies
- Sharing Jesus with people who have dementia
- Understanding and meeting the spiritual needs of residents
- Keeping the care team together
- Ministering to our grieving and dying friends
- Sharing Communion and other special services
- Maintaining good relations with nursing home staff
- Connecting with other nursing home ministries in the USA

You can encourage your team to read a chapter on their own and then come together to discuss what each has learned, and the ways this may be applied in your specific outreach.

Another approach is to copy a few pages (from a book or website) that cover a specific topic of concern, and give it to your team members to read and discuss. There are copyright issues with this, so please be careful. (Note: You are welcome to copy up to 10 pages from any God Cares Ministry materials to share with care team members. Please acknowledge the source.)

A few other books I have appreciated are:

ALL THE DAYS OF MY LIFE – The Sonshine Society

A CUP OF COLD WATER – Sharon Henning

A HANDBOOK FOR NURSING HOME MINISTRY – Christian Concourse

BUILDING A MINISTRY FOR HOMEBOUND and NURSING HOME RESIDENTS – Marie White Webb

NURSING HOME MINISTRY – Chong Sung Lee

Such books could make a great gift for birthday, appreciation, etc.

Goal #2   Provide the training

There are a few issues to be considered when providing a training program for your team:

- What kind of training (live, video, books)
- When and where you will host it
- Will you provide refreshments, workbooks, etc.
- What will the costs be

I recommend you talk with your pastor about all of these. You will also do well to involve your team with planning your training. They can help you promote the ministry among other church members (possible recruits) and even invite members of other churches who might be willing to establish their own nursing home outreach.

Possible hurdle: Be very careful that you or your team members are not too busy with administrative tasks during the training programs. This distraction has been very counter-productive for some. Therefore, I recommend that you seek help from other church members to handle refreshments and logistics during the actual training program.

If your team is planning to provide group ministry, plan to assign "ministry positions" for each volunteer. (See Appendix B for recommended descriptions.) It is profitable to provide each volunteer with a brief, written description of his responsibilities, schedule, and the team leader's phone number if there is a need to cancel or ask further questions.

Extra mile tip: Consider sending an invitation to your Activities Director to attend the training program. Her involvement will help to deepen relationships and potentially open more doors of opportunity. Also, invite your pastor to give the opening welcome and the prayer at the first session.

Goal # 3   Apply the principles you were taught

Experience is also a great teacher. No one becomes a skillful swimmer by reading a book or attending a seminar. We have to jump in and apply the things we are taught. As a leader, you can watch for team members who are applying the principles from the training, they can become great mentors to the inexperienced. Their coaching opportunities will increase their fulfillment and the overall fruitfulness of your spiritual garden.

Soapbox tip: Whatever approach you choose, I strongly urge that each team member receive ongoing Bible-based training. I cannot over-emphasize this need. Most overseas missionaries study and prepare for years. They must understand the language, the culture, and unique ways to bear fruit among the people-group to whom they are sent. There are many who choose not to take the time to read, attend seminars, or team-up with experienced and fruitful missionaries in the care centers. It is the residents who ultimately lose out because of such neglect.

I will get off my soap box in just a minute, but let me say just one more thing. If you or your team could learn one more principle that would cause you to become better servants for our Lord, and enable you to be more fruitful for His glory, would it be worth the investment of time or finances? I have watched countless volunteers (even very experienced ones) become more effective and relaxed and even liberated from unnecessary challenges after learning Biblical principles for effective nursing home ministry. You are welcome to put a guilt trip on the prideful one who thinks otherwise. . .

OK, I'll behave now.

Check list:

- ☐ I have reviewed the training resources at www.GodCaresMinistry.com
- ☐ I have previewed the recruiting videos that I received after adding my ministry to the list of ministry friends
- ☐ I have consulted with my pastor and team members regarding the method, date, and location of training we will use
- ☐ I have received funds from church or team members to purchase training materials
- ☐ I have purchased training materials
- ☐ I have invited other church members to participate in the training and sent a reminder to each one
- ☐ I have invited the Activities Director to participate in the training
- ☐ Our experienced team members are helping younger Christians apply the training principles we are learning

Phase five Scriptures to study:

2Peter 1:5-8   *2Timothy 2:15*

Acts 4:13   *Acts 6:1-7*

Notes: _____

_____

_____

_____

_____

_____

_____

_____

_____

_____

_____

_____

_____

_____

_____

_____

_____

_____

_____

_____

_____

_____

_____

PHASE SIX:

Protecting and supporting the plants

Now that your team has been trained and given clear focus, you will begin to see how this garden takes on a life of its own. It is a joy to watch how God causes all team members to bear unique fruit according to their gifts, and how much the residents are nourished by it. There are however, a few gardening items to consider. Plants continue to need water, fertilization and the most fruitful ones will need added support. Also, if weeds crop up, you will need to pull them out without harming the roots of the good plants.

Keep watch over yourselves and all the flock of which the Holy Spirit has made you overseers. (Acts 20:28)

There are a number of ways to maintain your spiritual garden in the nursing home. But in this phase, I would like to encourage just one primary principle; *learn servant-leadership*. Servant-leadership does not seek to force plants to bear fruit; rather, it asks the question, what can I do to cultivate a healthy and encouraging environment for each of my team members?

Extra mile tip: After your care team receives training and is assigned ministry positions, I highly recommend that you ask your pastor to pray over them before the church. Those who complete the <u>LIVING WATERS</u> training sessions are eligible to receive a Certificate of Completion. This can be presented by the pastor when he gives his public blessing. This is a very Biblical form of spiritual covering that provides significant protection and encouragement.

We can all learn a lot from the parables Jesus taught in the following verses. Please take the time to meditate on these during your quiet times with the Lord. They hold many principles for maintaining the Lord's garden.

Matthew 13:1-43, Mark 4:1-34, Luke 8:4-15, Luke 13:6-9, Luke 13:18-21, John 15:1-17

After a person has begun work as a volunteer, he must not be taken for granted. We find it extremely profitable to invest time in building both individual relationships and also team relationships. Jesus modeled this by often withdrawing to spend time alone with His disciples. Relationships need to be cultivated and nurtured. Below are several helpful suggestions that we have learned over the years. Some are a reminder of what I have already shared in this guidebook and some will add to your knowledge.

- Encourage team members by spending time with them outside your time together in the nursing homes. Encourage them with cards, an occasional phone call, or a meeting over coffee. Pray for your team members. Be aware of their special needs and tell them that you are praying for them.

- Remember that teams that visit weekly in one nursing home stay together longer than those who visit several homes monthly.

- Provide support meetings for open discussion, topical instruction, the sharing of experiences and any prayer requests. These meetings will give team members an opportunity to communicate concerns and desires. Let them know that their input is very important.

- One of the things we do in Ohio is provide an annual banquet for all nursing home ministry volunteers. We call this event, **Power Night**, because our goal is to encourage and empower these special servants. In addition to a catered meal, we provide inspirational speakers, testimonies from the audience, ministry resource displays

63

and prayer. It is a great supportive time for all! You are welcome to join us. See our newsletters for current details.

- It should be expected that a certain percentage of volunteers who begin with great enthusiasm will drop out shortly after they start. There are many possible reasons which may include: a change in one's personal situation which makes volunteering impossible, a misunderstanding of what was required, or "it just is not for me" reasons. In most cases, the volunteer can be made more comfortable if assigned to a different task.

- Be a servant. If a person stops going to a nursing home, instead of asking why and pressuring him to come back, sensitively explore the reasons for dropping out and, if possible, eliminate obstacles by providing any needed support. Some people may need to drop out of the ministry for a season only and then return when family or personal circumstances permit.

- Be willing to make adjustments and changes as team members offer suggestions that might enhance the team's effectiveness.

- Invest time in learning the strengths of various team members and use them in ministry. Step back so others can step forward. People flourish best when they minister using their gifts and strengths. This does not mean, however, we will never have to do things we do not like to do.

- It is a blessing to know we are depended on and appreciated by each other.

- Accountability is important but effective only when team members have previously understood *and* agreed on what is expected of them.

- A volunteer appreciation/recognition program can be a great source of encouragement. Articles in the church newsletter, bulletin board displays, years-of-service pins,

or gifts during special annual luncheons or dinners, are all possible ways of building up the faithful care team servants. Most Christians do not minister for praise or rewards; however, all of us appreciate being thanked and valued by friends. Honor people for work well done with all sincerity.

- Update your pastor periodically by letter or report. It is normal for pastors not to know the full details of your ministry. Therefore, you cannot assume your pastor will know when you have special needs and challenges. Many pastors work from the no-news-is-good-news policy, so let him know the good and the bad news. *A good friend of mine, Sharon Henning, leads a nursing home ministry in a very large church. She sends a monthly "Good News Report" to her pastor. Her pastor occasionally quotes some of the testimonies of what God is doing through this special ministry.*

- Many of the seeds of love and faith that you sow may seem insignificant, but remember what God can do with a tiny mustard seed *(Mark 4:31-32).*

- When a church adopts a care center, they will have a core group who will visit the home three or four times a month. Once a quarter, or so, the church can also provide special services from the choir, youth ministry, drama team, etc. Many such events are mentioned in NURSING HOME MINISTRY, and not all of them need to be religious in nature. These will help to involve the entire church in the adoption process, and are also great opportunities to recruit new team members. Be sure to have your team prepared and praying for more special workers.

When Jesus saw the crowds, he had compassion on them, because they were harassed and helpless, like sheep without a shepherd. Then he said to his disciples, "The harvest is plentiful but the workers are few. Ask the Lord of the harvest, therefore, to send out workers into his harvest field" (Matthew 9:36-38)

- Remember, you are asking people to give one of life's most valued resources-Time. The potential team members will need to sense that there is a genuine need and a specific plan to meet the need.

> ***Be devoted to one another in brotherly love. Honor one another above yourselves.***
> ***Romans 12:10***

Notes: _____

_____

_____

_____

_____

_____

_____

_____

_____

_____

_____

_____

_____

_____

_____

_____

Notes: _____

PHASE SEVEN:

Enjoying the fruit

As your team becomes well established in the ways of Christ, and in caring relationships, you will see this garden bear much fruit. If you remain faithful and prayerful, you can expect that residents as well as team members will grow in faith, and experience the hope and peace of Jesus. Such fruitfulness is evidence of God's blessing.

Land that drinks in the rain often falling on it
and that produces a crop useful to those for
whom it is farmed receives the blessing of God.
Hebrews 6:7

My heart is filled with memories of men and women who became dear friends. They confided in me with deep and personal issues, we looked to the Lord's word, prayed together and found the grace of God to press on. I know that many of these friends are now with Jesus and I look forward to the day we will all be together.

Some of the fruit I have enjoyed

Taste and see that the Lord is good. . . Psalm 34:8

The changes that took place in my friends' lives are part of the fruit of our team's spiritual garden. Let me share a few bites:

There was Ken, who told us that when he first entered the nursing home that he was planning to find a way to commit suicide. After several weeks of attending our Bible study and then being baptized, Ken changed. He often told me that one of

68

the best things that ever happened to him was coming to live in this nursing home, because this is where he found the Lord. He lived there for 5 or 6 years and was greatly loved by all the residents and staff.

Gladys was already a Christian when she came into the home. She really loved Jesus and wanted to serve Him. One of the things she would do was take attendance at the worship services. She made sure we did not forget any of the residents. Even with her limitations and inability to get around, she made a major impact on many residents throughout the nursing home.

When I met Rachel, she was very disappointed with her family and could not figure out why God would make her live in "this place". After a few visits, I convinced her to read a Bible that I brought in for her. She was a real blessing! When I would visit her, she would ask me questions that she had written out while reading the Bible during the week. A few years before she died, she organized a small chapel time so that other residents could ask Bible / religious questions. At least two people were saved as a result of our times together.

Helen gave her heart to Jesus (I believe at one of our services). She loved the Bible studies so much that she would not eat her dinner on the nights we would come. When asked about this, she explained that she had a colostomy and did not want to attend to it and miss the Bible study after dinner.

Jean is an 82-year old lady on our care team. She loves to play the piano. She often needs a ride to the nursing home, and has a hard time walking. She has become a major blessing to all of us, as she leads us in worship and singing of the old hymns. Her gratitude often beams from her face, because she feels privileged to participate in our Bible fellowship time.

Chaz, a construction worker, is one of our team members. Recently, during our prayer time, just before the worship services, he explained how his day was filled with difficult challenges and that he had no strength. We prayed that the Lord would use him in spite of his weaknesses. At the end of the evening we regathered for our usual share-time before going home. Chaz was lit up with energy! He told us about his visit with Mary and how the Lord opened her heart to receive Him as her Lord and Savior. I explained that I had been sharing the Gospel with her for over ten years and she had been unwilling to surrender to Christ. We praised God for helping Chaz go the extra mile, even when he felt like staying home to rest. The following Tuesday, when we arrived for our service, the nurse told us that Mary had passed away on Sunday. What a sobering thought to realize how close our friends are to eternity's door. And what a blessing it is for us to have assurance that our sister Mary is now with her Lord!

All these people were blessed and became a blessing by faith in Jesus. Our efforts to help them and share God's Love and Word with them made a significant impact in their lives. I have so many more stories that I could tell, but I just don't have the room to tell about Clarence, Henry, Pat, Frank, Marie, Bob, and Marilyn, who all found life in Christ. Some entered the nursing home hardened by religious legalism. Some attended church all their lives, but never had a personal relationship with Jesus. And some were believers, yet had their faith shaken by the transition from a comfortable home to the care facility. All these and many more became treasures to me and the other residents.

> *. . .if you spend yourselves in behalf of the hungry and satisfy the needs of the oppressed, then your light will rise in the darkness, and your night will become like the noonday. The LORD will guide you always; he will satisfy your needs in a sun-scorched land and will strengthen your frame. You will be like a well-watered garden, like a spring whose waters never fail. (Isaiah 58:10-11)*

Watch and pray

Jesus said, *"Look at the fig tree and all the trees" (Luke 21:29).* He said this so that we would apply everyday practical principles to the workings of the Kingdom of Heaven.

Throughout this guidebook I have likened nursing home ministry to gardening. As you can see, there are many parallels between the two. If you experience a lack of fruit in your spiritual garden, I highly encourage you to go sit in a fruitful vegetable or flower garden, talk to the gardener, and watch for the parallel answers to your concerns. Ask the Lord to reveal what caused the natural garden you are sitting in to flourish; and what it will take to cause your spiritual garden at the nursing home to do the same. Perhaps you will see an area where you need to adjust, or perhaps there is a seasonal change that you need only to persevere through faithfully.

I hope this guidebook has been helpful for you. I want you to know that I am praying for you. As your team reaches out to bless the residents, I am sure that you will be amazingly blessed in return. I am greatly encouraged by the testimonies of those who have planted their nursing home ministry garden and would love to hear from you. Also, if you should encounter a need, do not hesitate to contact the office of God Cares Ministry. Let us pray with you and seek guidance from the Lord of the harvest. We are here to serve you.

May Jesus bless you greatly as you abide in Him.

God Cares Ministry

515 Moore Road, Suite 3, Avon Lake, Ohio 44012
Phone & Fax: (440) 930-2173   info@GodCaresMinistry.com
www.GodCaresMinistry.com

Handbook: NURSING HOME MINISTRY Where Hidden Treasures Are Found

Newsletter: "God Cares News", six issues each year

Support fund: Equipment & resource funds

Training video: Living Waters in a Dry Land

Recruiting and training preview videos

Power Night: Our annual banquet to encourage and empower nursing home missionaries

The SonShine Society

Po Box 327 Lynnwood, WA 98046-0327
425-353-4732   www.sonshinesociety.org

Giant Print Materials: Song books, Scripture portions, Tracts, Cards, and Devotionals

Music: CDs/cassette tapes with words to accompany song books

Training Materials: Training guide, two-part basic training video

Newsletter: "Bits of SONshine", five issues each year

Faithful Friends
www.Faithfulfriends.org   This website has links to many helpful nursing home ministries and resources

Christian Concourse

1543 Norcova Ave. Norfolk, VA 23502   757-714-3133
www.christianconcourse.org   Jerry@christianconcourse.org

Handbook for Nursing Home Ministry

Large print hymn book: with accompanying instrumental CDs

Christian Poetry

~~~~~~~~

Christian Fellowship of Care Center Ministries
www.CFCCM.net

This is a fellowship of Christians who lead a nursing home ministry in their region, helping church groups to develop outreaches in care centers. We gather annually to network and provide mutual support. The website provides a link to more than 20 such ministries in the USA.

You are encouraged to contact one of the participating CFCCM ministries nearest you.

Nursing Home Chaplaincy:

Currently there are three Christ-centered chaplaincy groups that I can recommend. There is another Christ-centered chaplaincy group in its development stages. I trust they will have a link on CFCCM.net once it is up and running. The three are as follows:

Community Chaplain Services

PO Box 117 Foxboro, MA 02035-0117   508-543-0322
www.communitychaplainservices.org   commchap@verizon.net

Love Your Neighbor

PO Box 1886 Gresham, OR 97030
www.lyn.org   daveclyn@comcast.net

Nursing Home Ministries

PO Box 22246 Portland, OR 97269-2246
www.nursinghomeministries.com   nhminc@comcast.net

~~~~~~~

If Nursing Home Ministry is your life-calling:

If you desire to develop a nursing home ministry to help the churches in *your region* adopt nursing homes, it would be my honor to personally help you. As the Lord has allowed me to help start care teams, He is also allowing me to help start regionally focused ministries like God Cares Ministry. If you sense the Lord is calling you to develop such an outreach, I recommend you take the same first steps outlined in chapter two of this guidebook, and then call me as you begin step three, 440-930-2173.

Chaplain Bill Goodrich

APPENDIX B   A nursing home ministry care team

CARE TEAMS are normally made up of four to eight Christians who adopt one nursing home and visit the residents on a regular basis. We seek to establish caring relationships with all residents in the home. Our sincere friendships often result in helping them find hope, peace, and purpose in Jesus. Below are brief descriptions of the five different positions that make up a Nursing Home Ministry Care Team. Sometimes a person will take on more than one of these positions. This is fine, because our goal is to enable each team member to discover, use, and grow in his/her gifts and skills. The positions are as follows:

Team Coordinator: This person keeps the team together by communicating, praying with and for the team members, and coordinating an occasional team fellowship hour to encourage and strengthen the team members. This person is also the one who would maintain any needed records and also be the communication link between the Team Members, the Activities Director, and the Church Leadership.

Teacher: This person is responsible to pray for and prepare a message for a church service or Bible study. The message is usually a short devotional but can be a 30-minute Bible-study class that follows a time of worship and praise. NURSING HOME MINISTRY has two chapters dedicated to help teachers prepare and share life-giving messages.

Song Leader: This person is responsible to prepare and lead the group singing. This is usually about twenty minutes long at the beginning of a group service. The song leader can lead using an instrument or special accompanying CD's and hymnals designed for Nursing Home Ministry. Sometimes two individuals share this responsibility, one playing the instrument while the other is the more visible song leader.

Helpers: These people are responsible to help the other team members accomplish their tasks. Helpers help bring residents to church services, assist with turning hymn book pages, take attendance, etc. The helpers' role on the Ministry Care Team is **<u>VERY IMPORTANT</u>** because they will help the services to flow smoothly. Many shy people have started out as helpers. After several months of involvement they move into other team positions, and blossom in their gifting.

Friendly Visitors: These people are willing to visit room-bound residents. They have a willingness to establish caring friendships by listening to and sharing with residents who are not willing or able to go to the church services. Through time, friendly visitors earn the respect to share God's word and prayer so that residents draw closer to Jesus.

I asked a nursing home resident, who was formerly a teacher, to read through the first draft of this guidebook. In addition to some great editing help, she concluded. "This manual is designed to help you pursue a workable, satisfying ministry program wherever you may find yourself."

I think she may have caught the vision. . .

For additional copies of this guidebook or other resources from God Cares Ministry such as:

Nursing Home Ministry - Where Hidden Treasures Are Found – A great handbook for the beginner as well as the very experienced nursing home missionary. With over 250 pages of Bible-based instruction, encouragement, and testimonies, you will find much help to develop or strengthen your nursing home ministry.

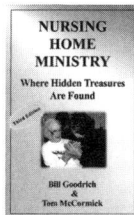

Living Waters in A Dry Land – A complete care team development curriculum to enable you to recruit, orient and train new volunteers and strengthen veteran nursing home missionaries. It includes everything you need to get a viable, life-giving nursing home ministry started, or to encourage and strengthen your existing outreach.

Recruiting videos – A DVD to assist you in recruiting Christians for nursing home ministry.

God Cares News – A bi-monthly newsletter written to encourage, inform, and instruct those interested in the nursing home mission field.

Contact

God Cares Ministry

515 Moore Road, Suite 3
Avon Lake, Ohio 44012
(440) 930-2173
www.GodCaresMinistry.com
info@GodCaresMinistry.com